EXPLORING GLOUCESTER, MASSACHUSETTS

Written and Illustrated by Alice Gardner

To the people of Gloucester of all ages on the occasion of the
city's 400+ anniversary (1623–2023). Thank you for your friendly, generous spirit
and love of your unique and beautiful community.

The City of Gloucester is located on the traditional and ancestral homeland of the Pawtucket people
and their neighbors the Massachusetts, Nipmuc, Penacook, and Wampanoag tribes. We recognize,
honor, and celebrate these native and indigenous peoples who have lived in this territory for more
than 10,000 years. Gloucester 400+ seeks to inspire future generations to honor the past and work
collectively to frame the future. Learn more about this project at gloucesterma400.org.

ISBN 979-8-218-06206-4

 Annisquam Lighthouse

Altar

Ardelle

Adventure

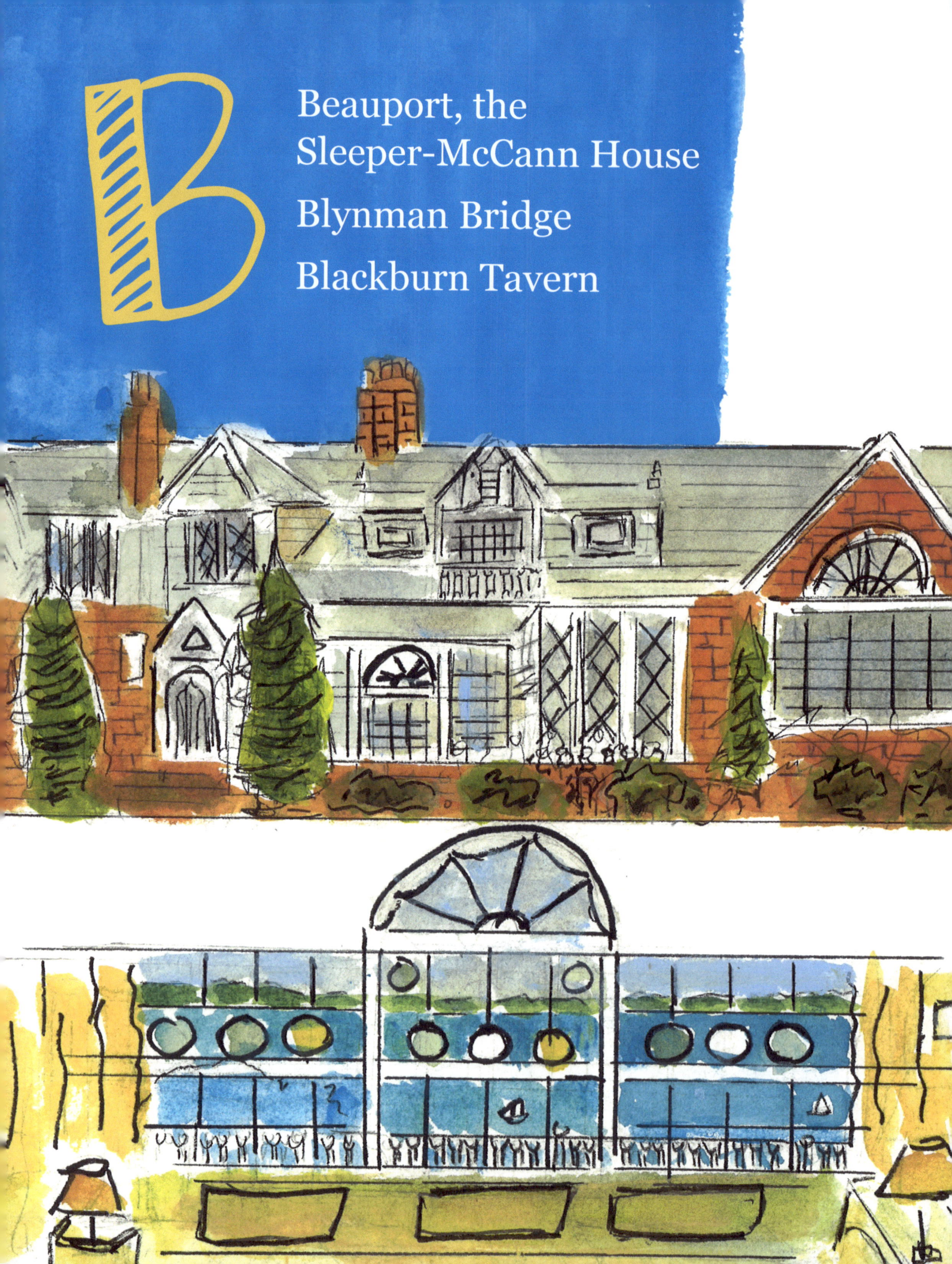

Beauport, the
Sleeper-McCann House

Blynman Bridge

Blackburn Tavern

BLYNMAN BRIDGE

1907

In honor of
Richard Blynman
First Minister and leading citizen
of Gloucester
who in 1643 dug this
canal uniting river and bay.

GHS

C

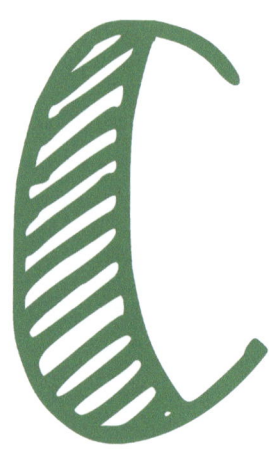

Cape Ann Museum

City Hall

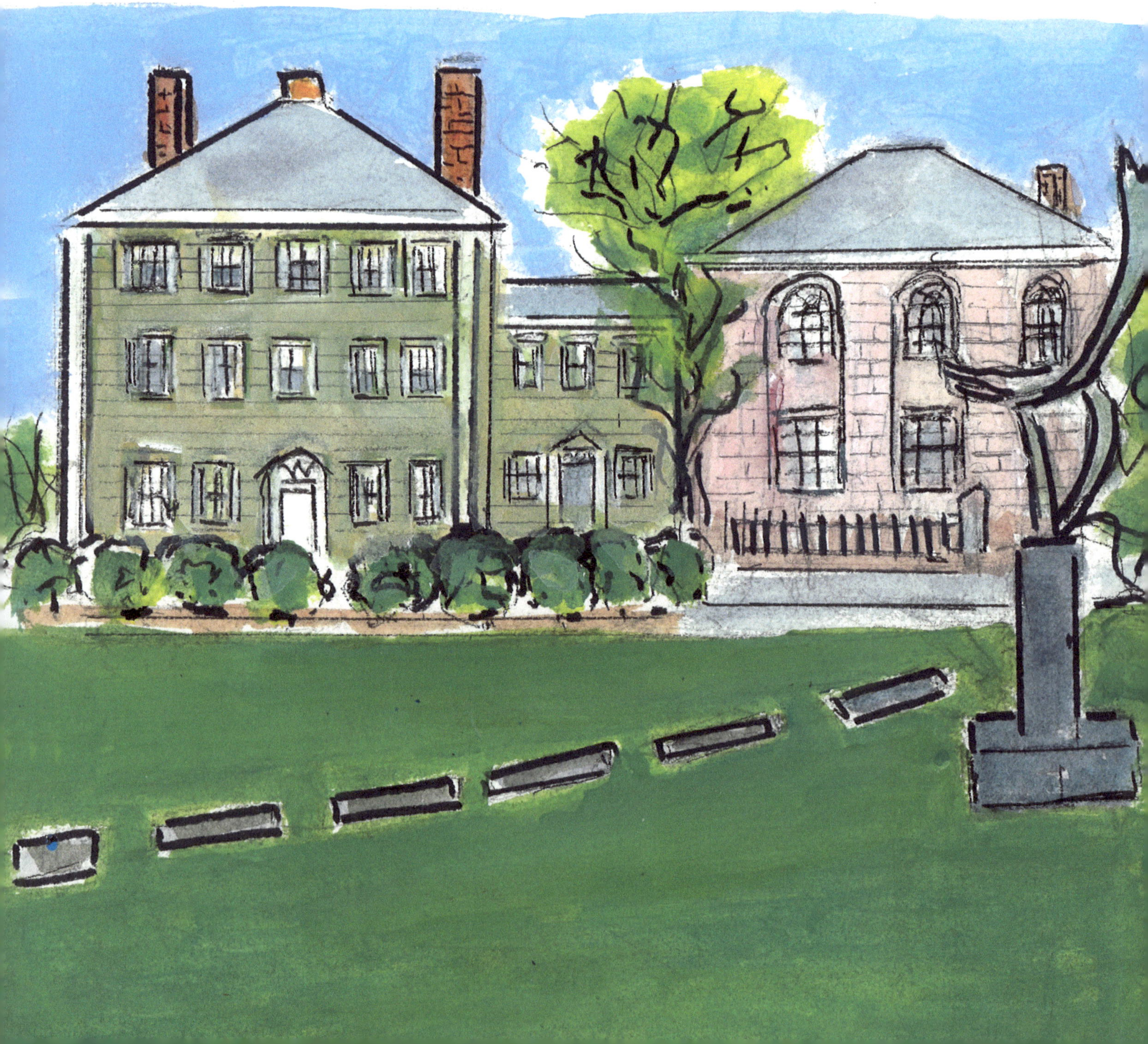

Dogtown Common

Dory Races

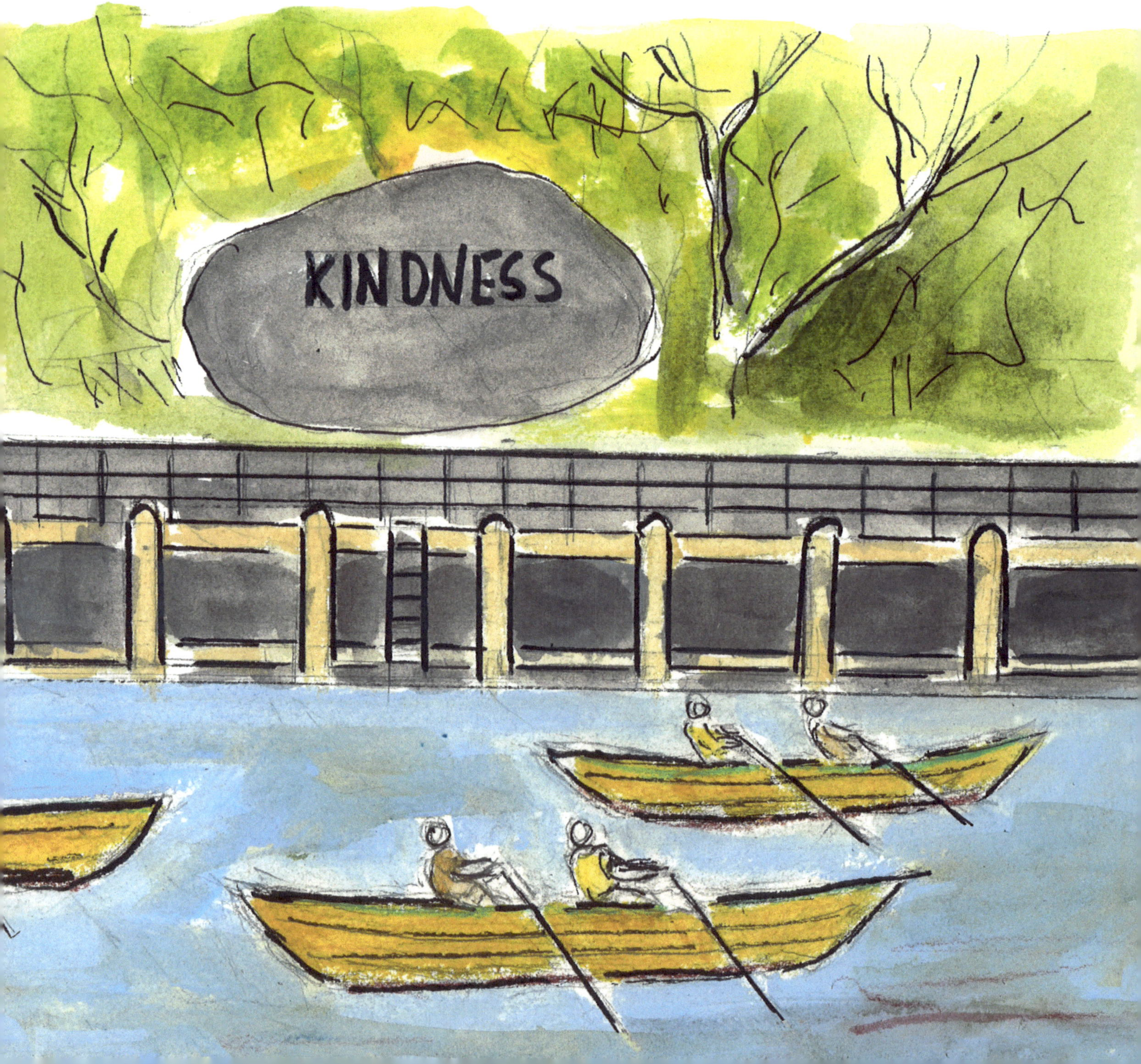

E

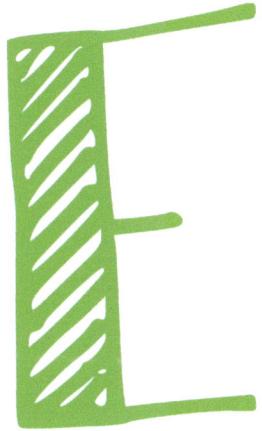

Eastern Point Lighthouse

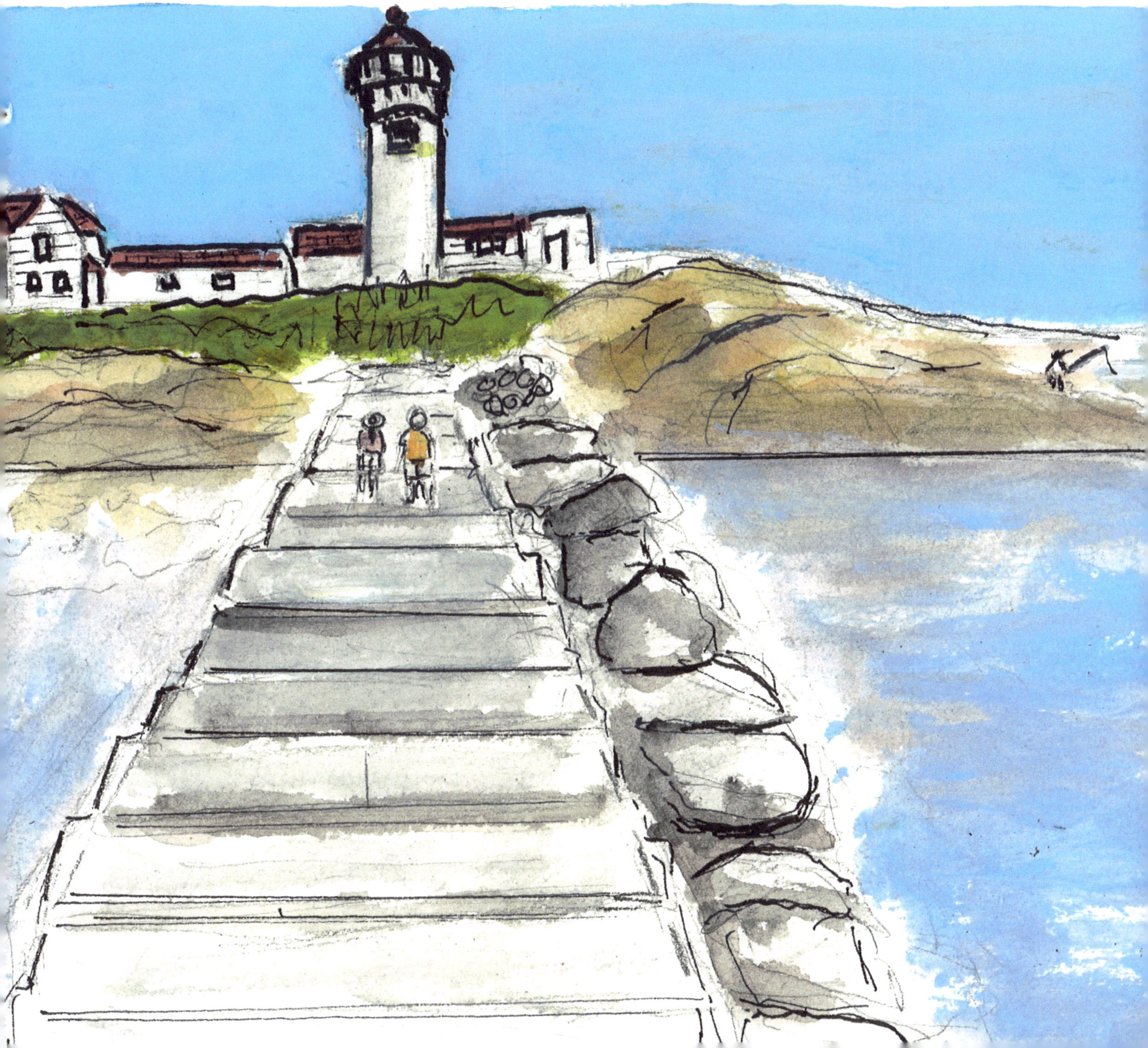

Fisherman's Memorial Statue

Fitz Henry Lane

Fishermen's Wives Memorial

Ferris Wheel

G

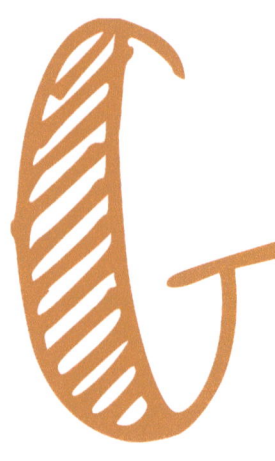

Good Harbor Beach

Greasy Pole

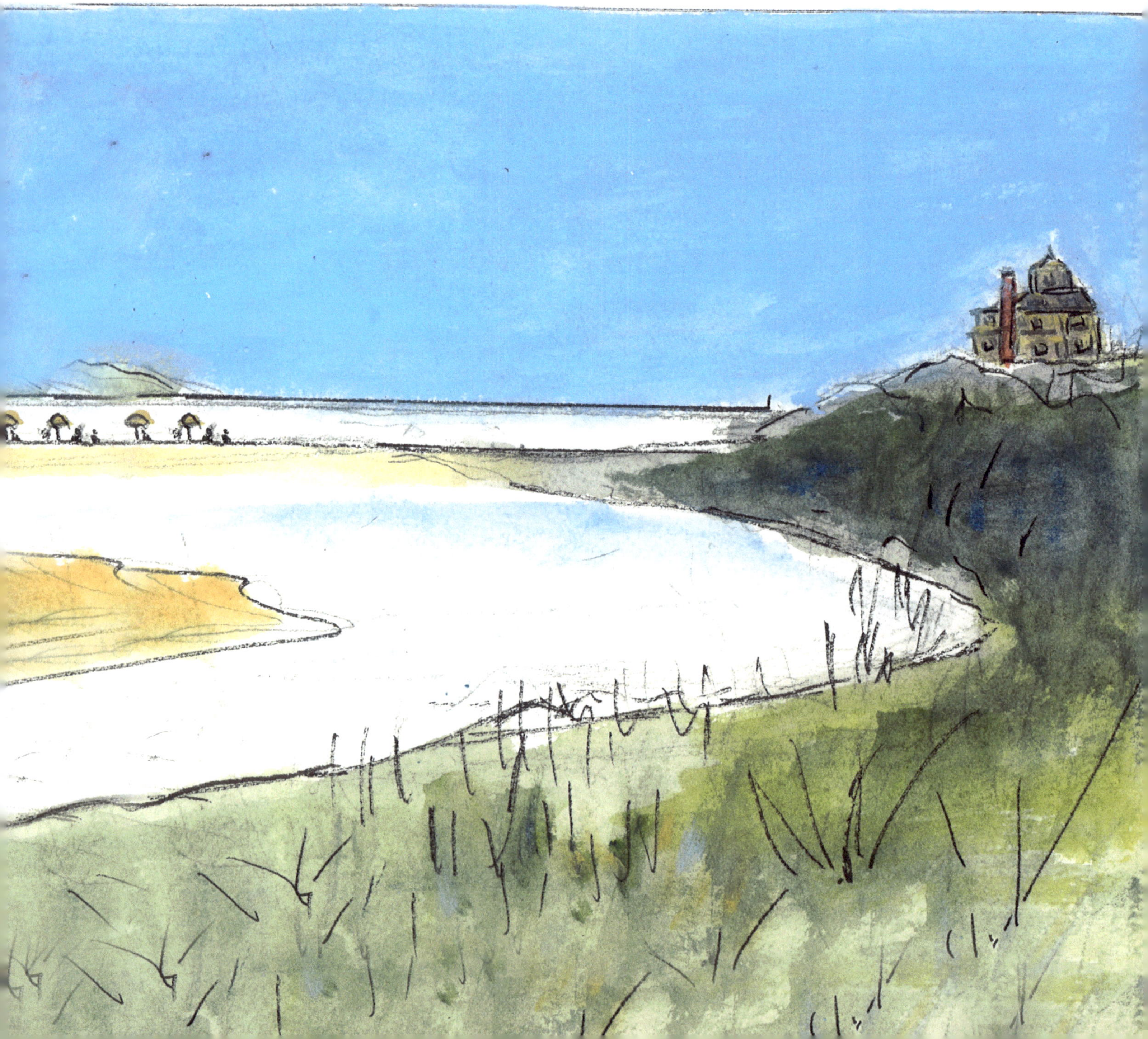

Hammond Castle
Harbor Walk

Story Posts on the Harbor Walk

1. St. Peter's
2. T. S. Elliott
3. Olson
4. Lobstering
5. Fishing Today
6. Salting Fish
7. H. Blackburn
8. Granite
9. Packing Fish
10. Magnolia
11. City Hall
12. Unitarian
13. Birding
14. Paint Factory
15. Nautical
16. Rocky Neck
17. C. Heberle
18. Fitz H. Lane
19. Sea Serpent
20. Our Lady
21. Schooner Adventure
22. Beauport
23. Dogtown
24. Dory
25. Railways
26. Norman's Woe
27. Gorton's
28. E. Hopper
29. W. Homer
30. V. L. Burton
31. S. Sawyer
32. Temple
33. C. Birdseye
34. J. S. Murray
35. St. Joseph's
36. Whales
37. Joan of Arc
38. Hammond Cast
39. Breakwater
40. R. Kipling
41. Fishermen's Wiv
42. Stage Fort Park

 Cape Pond Ice

Joan of Arc Statue

Jodrey State Fish Pier

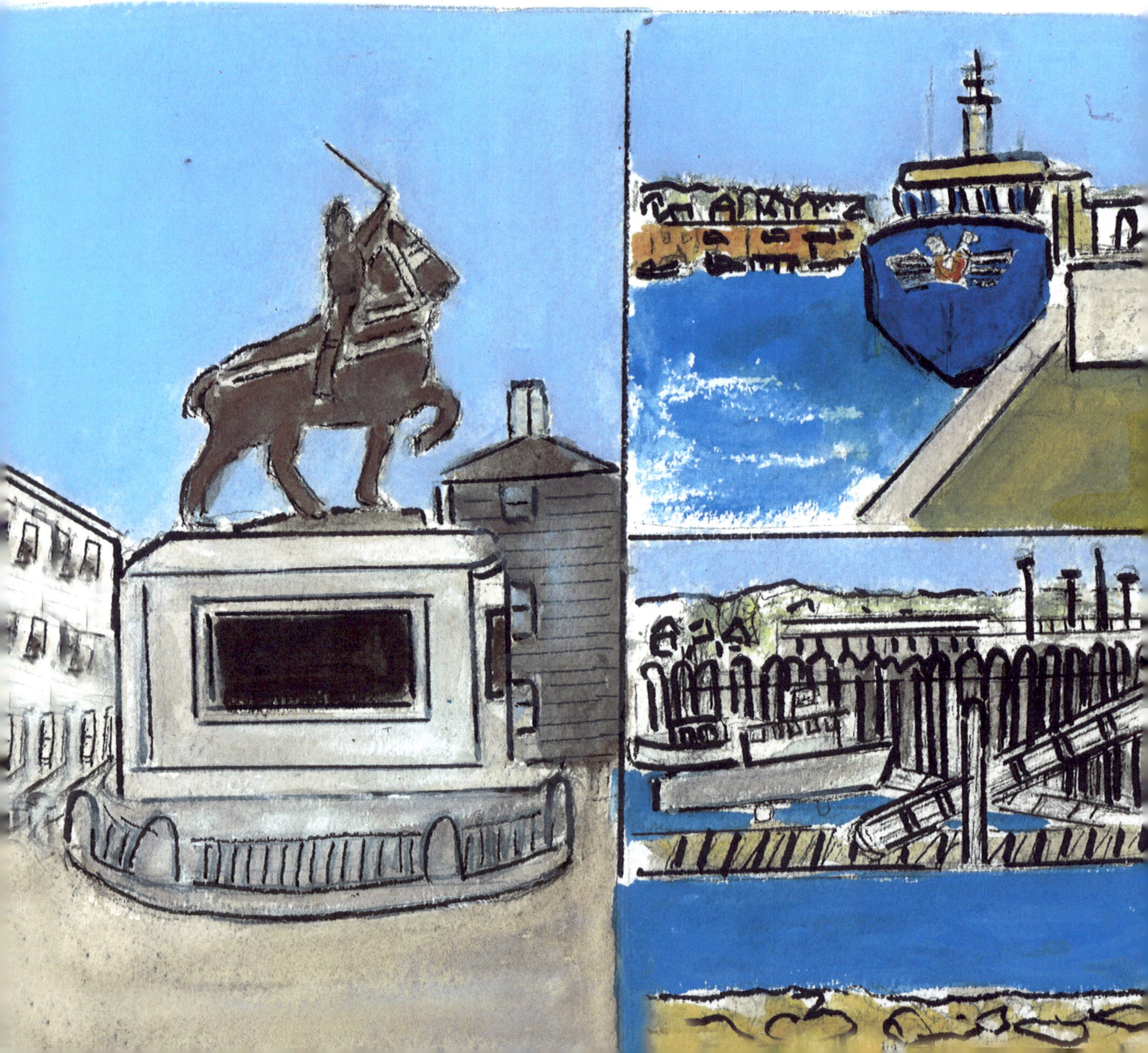

Keys to the Kingdom

Lobster Trap Tree

Maritime Gloucester

North Shore Arts Association

Novena

O

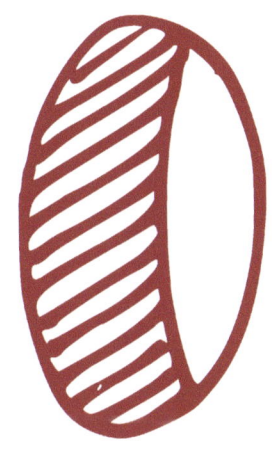

Our Lady of Good Voyage Church

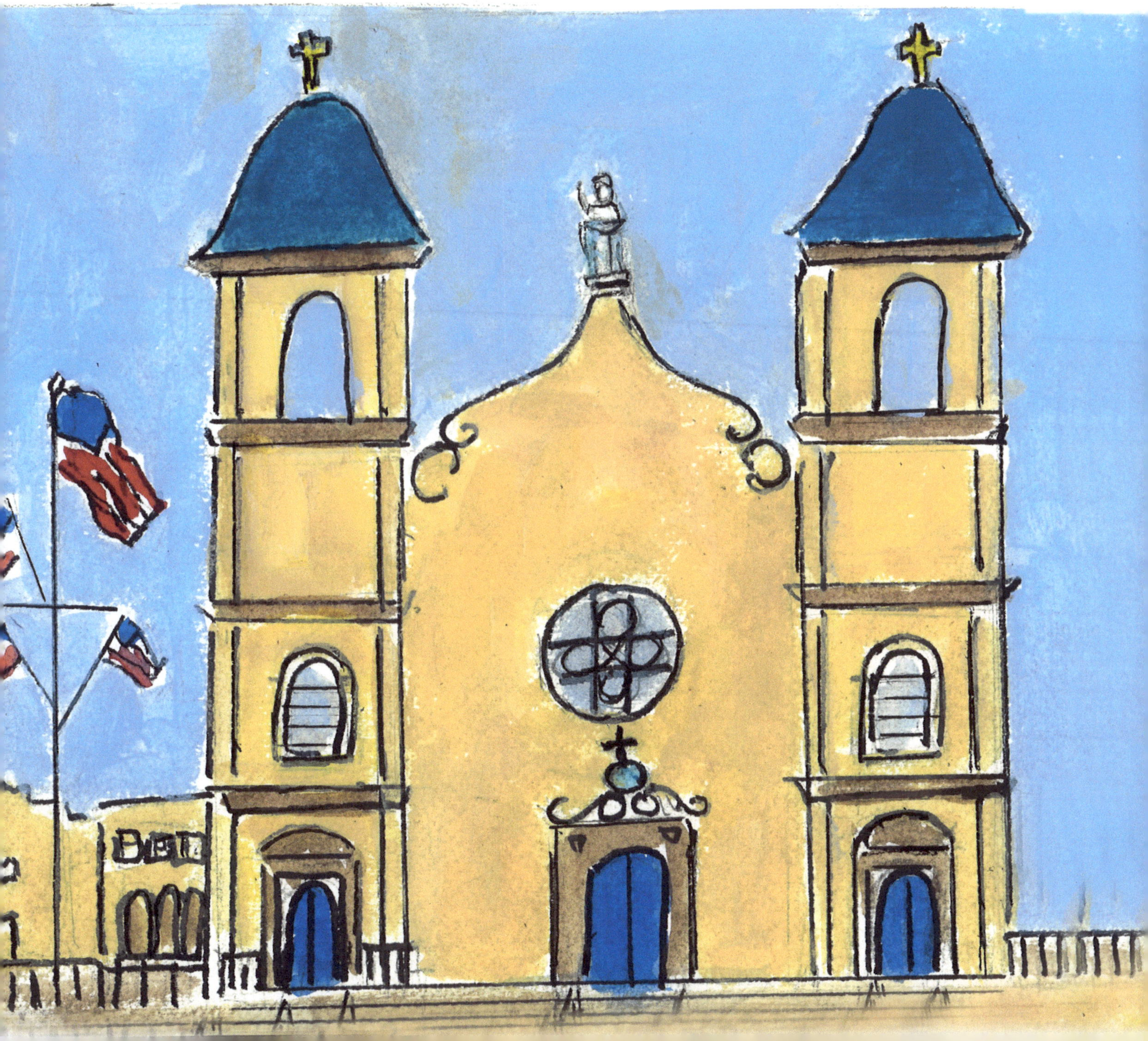

Princess Laura

Parade of Sail

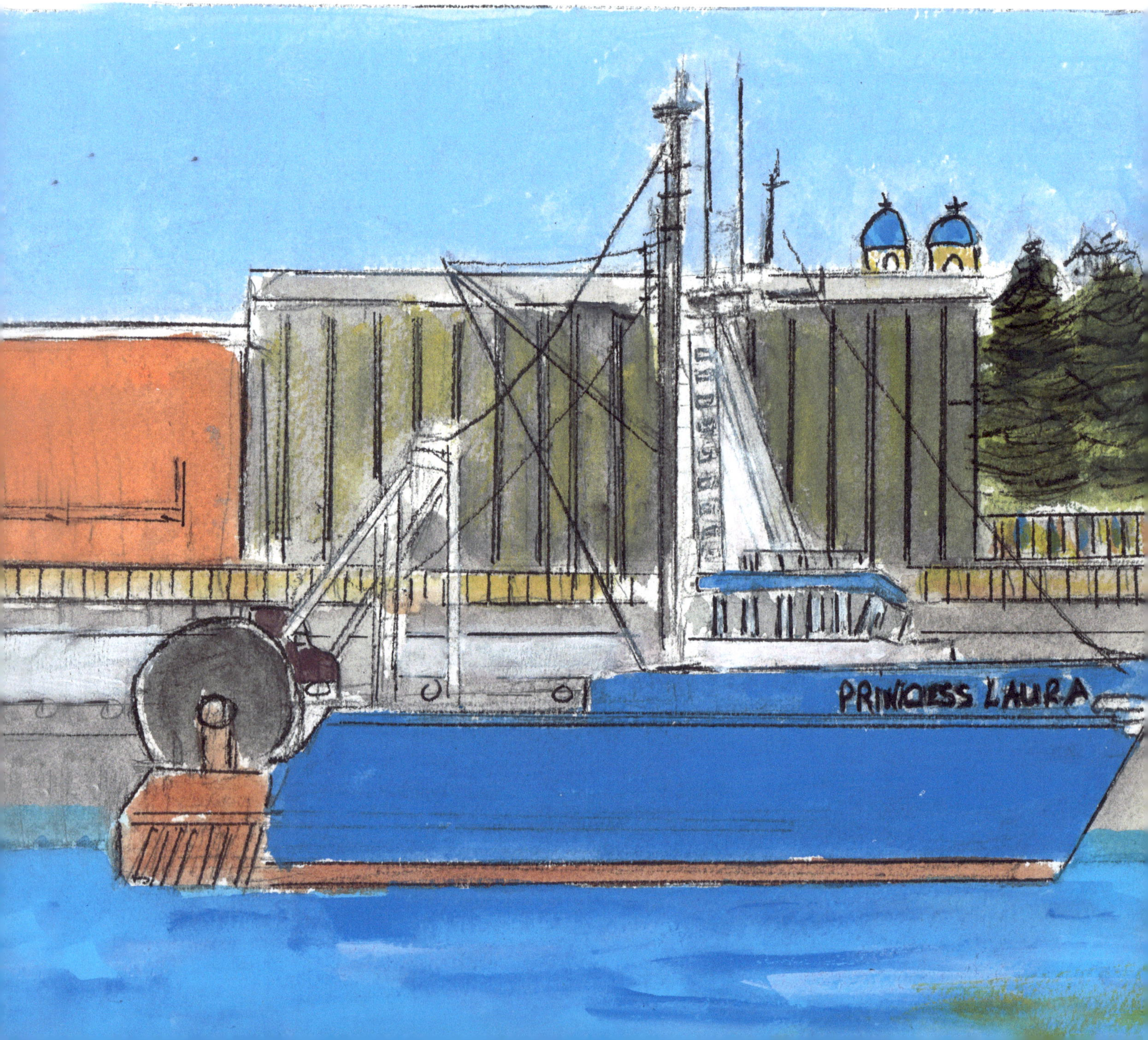

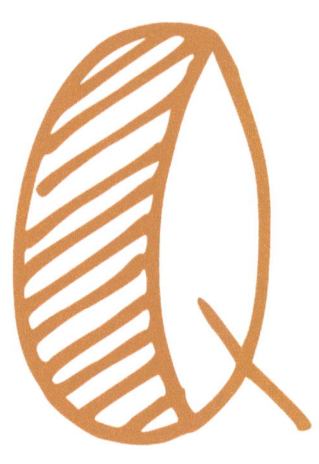

Quarry

Rocky Neck Art Colony
Ravenswood Park

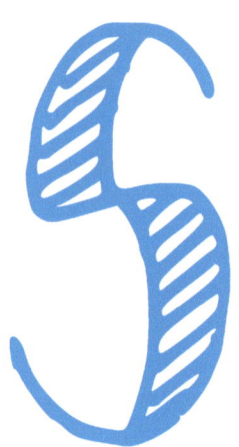

Sargent House Museum
Stage Fort Park
Seine Boat Races
Sea Serpent

Ten Pound Island Lighthouse

The Thomas E. Lannon

U

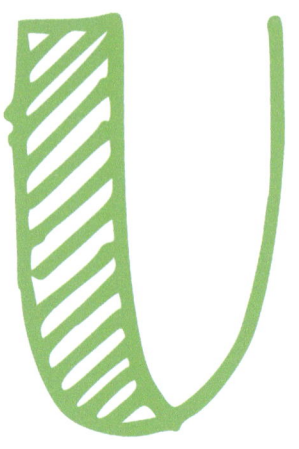

Unitarian Universalist Church

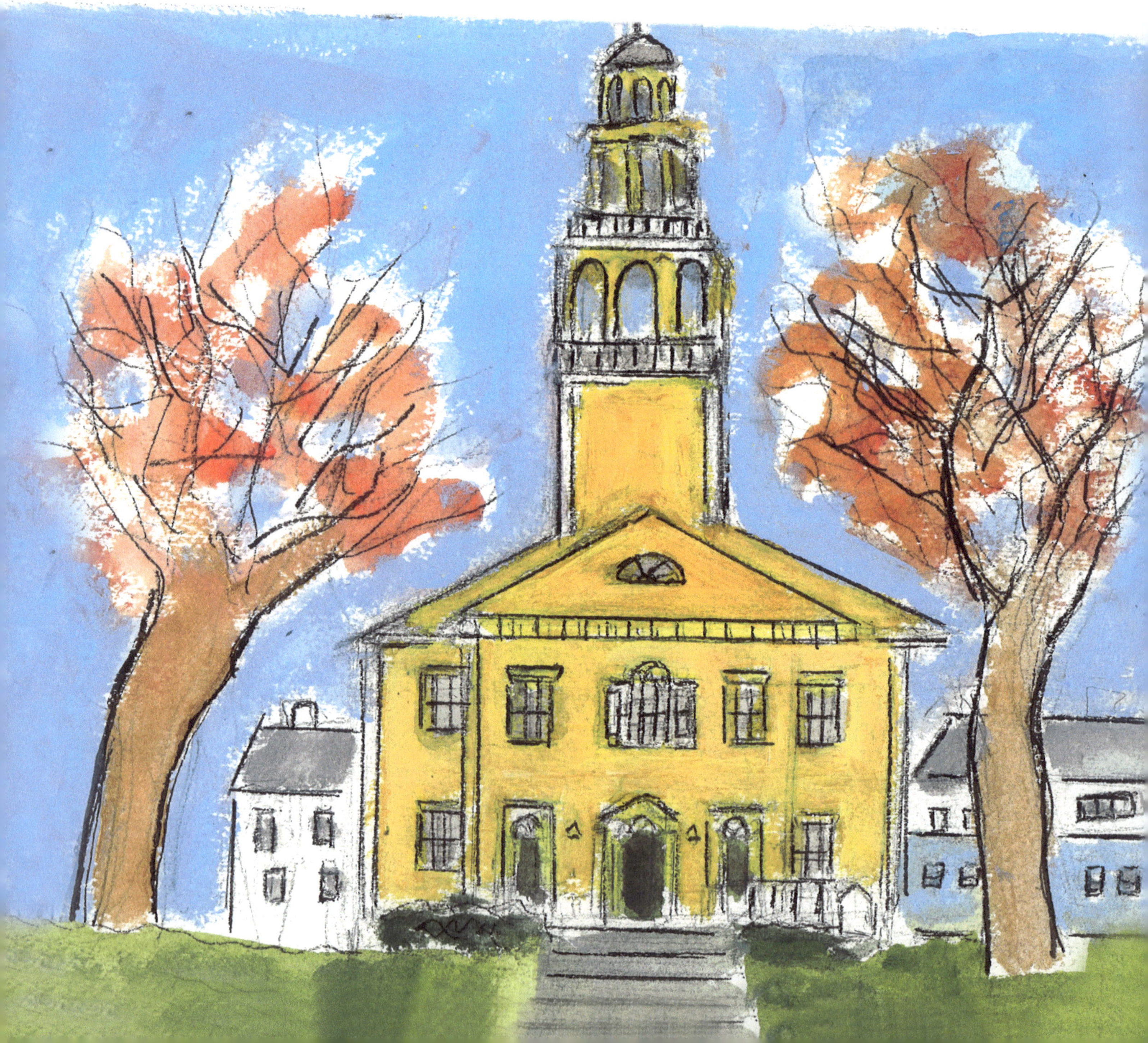

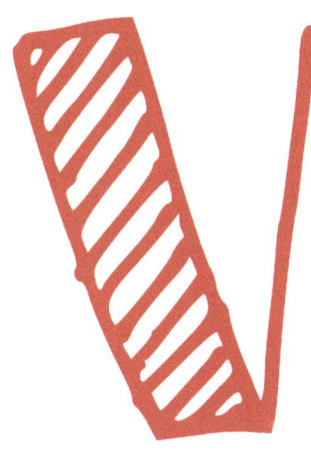

Viva San Pietro

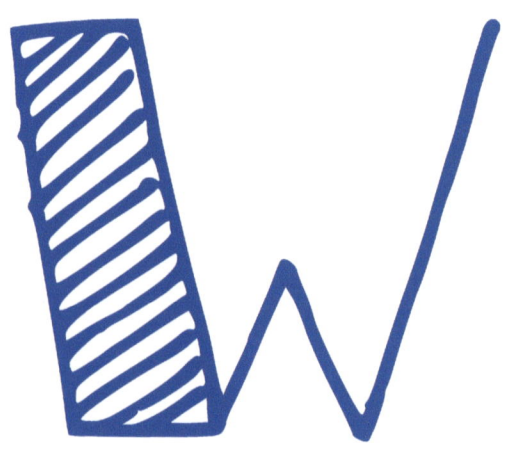

Wingaersheek Beach
Water Shuttle

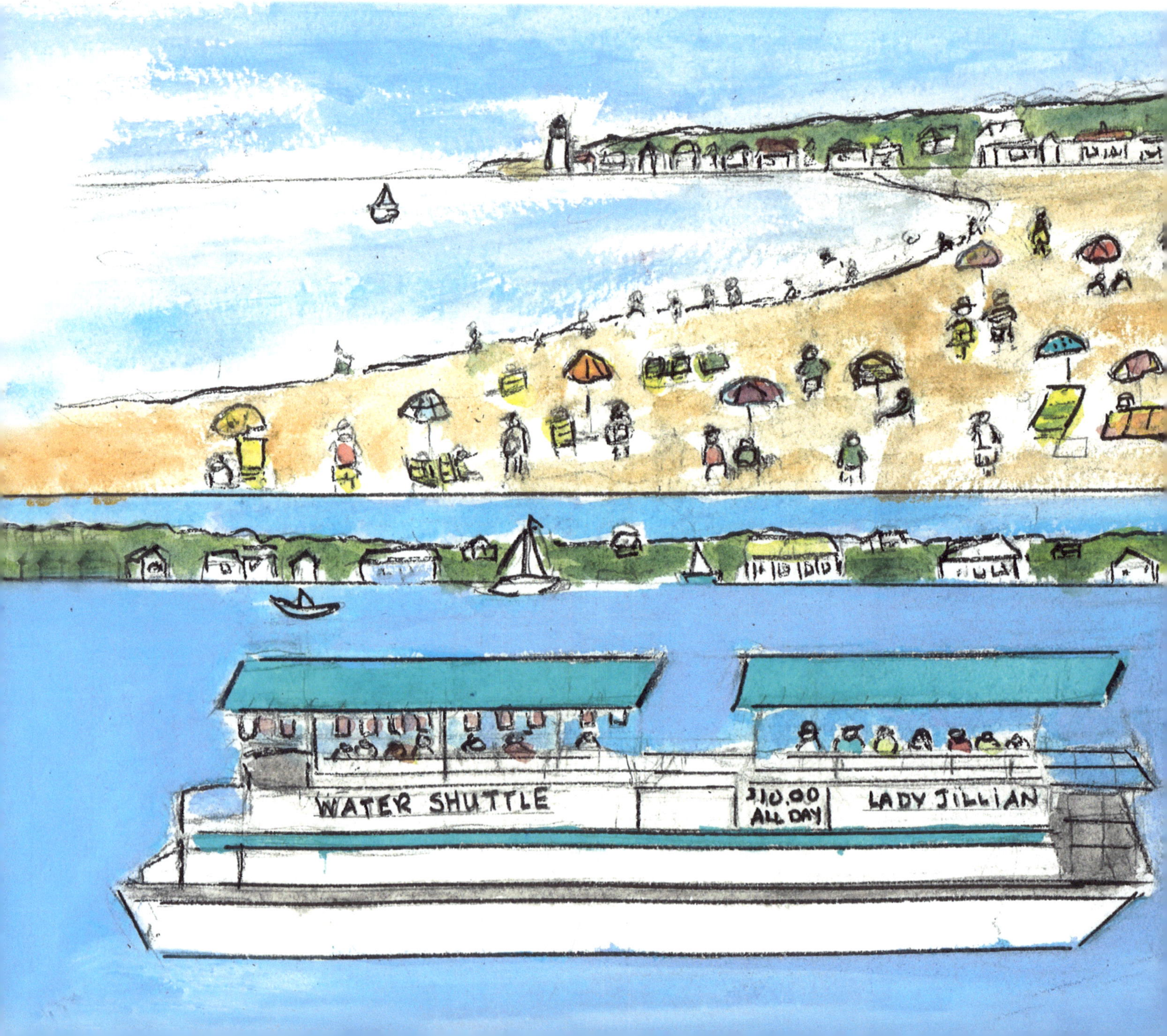

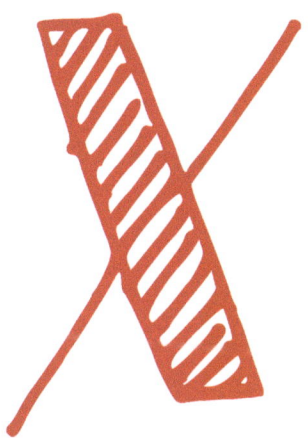

Xmas in Gloucester

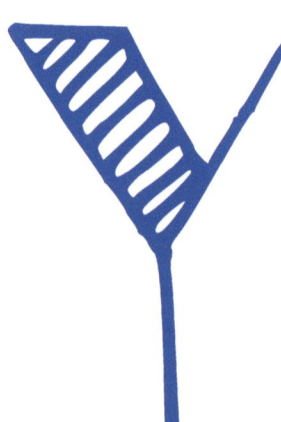

Yummy Italian Desserts

Occhi di Bue	Torta Della Nonna
Gelato	Pandoro
Cassata Siciliana	Cannoli
Tiramisu	Pizzelle

VIVA
San Pietro

Zuppa—Italian Minestrone

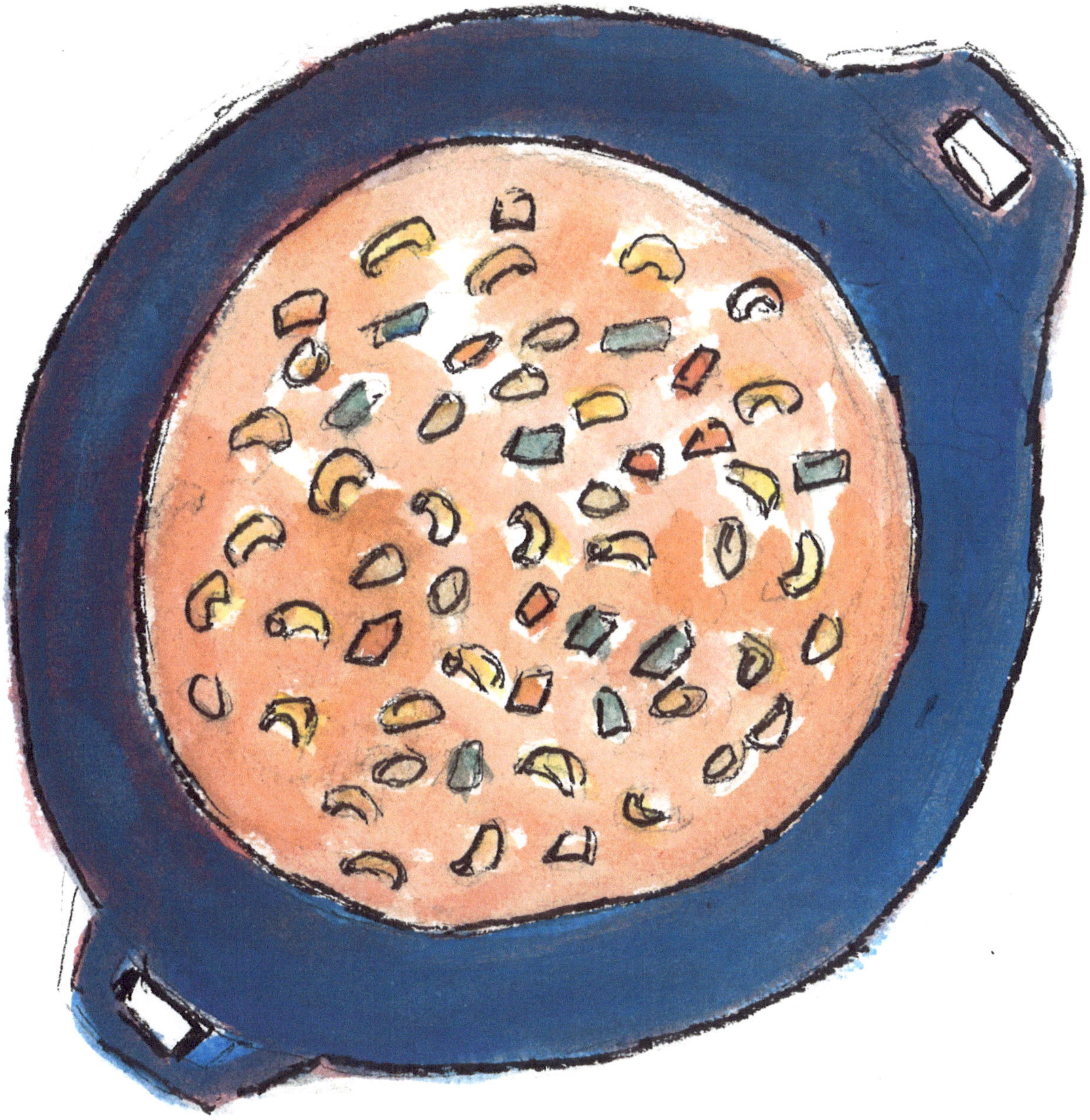

LET'S EXPLORE GLOUCESTER!

Gloucester has so much to offer! Below is just a sample of what you can explore. I hope you enjoy these adventures and many more!

VISITOR'S CENTERS

Visitor Welcoming Center, Stage Fort Park (24 Hough Avenue, discovergloucester.com).

Greater Cape Ann Chamber of Commerce (24 Harbor Loop, capeannchamber.com).

Beverly Service Plaza (Rt 128 North, Beverly). Many Cape Ann brochures and booklets are available at the Chamber of Commerce display.

ON THE WATER

Schooner Ardelle (23 Harbor Loop, 978-290-7168, schoonerardelle.com). Enjoy a peaceful sail around the harbor on the majestic *Ardelle*, a schooner berthed at the Harriet Webster Pier at Maritime Gloucester. Your ticket on the *Ardelle* gives you free admission to Maritime Gloucester (see below). Look for a seagull named "Mooch" who may visit the schooner looking for his favorite snack Cheetos. Known as the *"Pinky Schooner Ardelle"* for its pinched or pointed stern, the schooner was built by master ship builder Howard Burnham and his team of volunteers at H.A. Burnham Boat Building & Design in Essex. Howard is the 28th Burnham to operate a shipyard since 1819 and is the *Ardelle's* captain. The *Ardelle* was launched on July 9, 2011. Hundreds of people watched and cheered. Look for a video of the launch on YouTube!

Schooner Thomas E. Lannon (63 Rear Rogers Street, 978-281-6634, schooner. org). Another beautiful schooner, the *Lannon* is berthed at the pier next to the Gloucester House Restaurant. The *Lannon* was also built by Howard Burnham and was launched in 1997. If you're lucky, seagull Polly Five Toes might visit looking for a snack of oyster crackers from the schooner's captain; Polly Five Toes has been visiting the *Lannon* since 2013. A children's book by Sy Montgomery, *The Seagull and the Sea Captain*, tells the true story of Polly Five Toes and the friendship between the gull and the *Lannon's* Captain Heath Ellis. Join the crew for a sail and help hoist the masts while enjoying the many sights along the way!

Schooner Adventure (23 Harbor Loop, 978-281-8079, schooner-adventure.org). The grand schooner *Adventure* was built in 1926 and was a working wooden dory fishing schooner for 27 years until she was retired in 1953. During its tenure, the *Adventure* is reported to have caught the most fish of any fishing schooner—over 4 million dollars worth of cod, haddock, and halibut. After being used on Windjammer Cruises on the Maine coast, the *Adventure* was donated to the City of Gloucester in 1988 to be restored; she was 65 years young by then! The *Adventure* is now used as a floating classroom and for public sails. Watch *Schooner Adventure Dory Fishing* on YouTube to get a sense of what dory fishing was like when the *Adventure* first set sail!

Cape Ann Harbor Tours (978-283-1979, capeannharbortours.com). Choose from a variety of adventures below!

> **Gloucester Harbor Water Shuttle & Tour**. You can board the water shuttle at Harbor Loop at Solomon Jacobs Park or at Saint Peter's Landing. Get on and off all day or stay on for a full hour loop of the Harbor. The water shuttle stops at Rocky Neck (at the Studio Restaurant) and Cripple Cove (on demand only). Captain Steve fills you in on the unusual history of the area. You can see the *Wicked Tuna* boats and get a chance to see the working waterfront in action. One of the most cost-effective ways to see Gloucester by boat, your ticket is valid all day. No reservations necessary.

> **Lobstering/Harbor Tour**. This tour of Gloucester Harbor is 1.25 hours. You can see the Gloucester fishing fleet up close, as well as Ten Pound Island Lighthouse and Eastern Point Lighthouse. On the way, the crew will haul up a lobster trap and teach you about lobstering.

> **Lighthouse Cruise**. Enjoy a 2.5-hour cruise of Gloucester's entire harbor. See the fishing fleet and lighthouses up close and hear a fun historic narration as you go along.

Cape Ann Whale Watch (415 Main Street, 800-877-5110, seethewhales.com).

7 Seas Whale Watch (63 Rogers Street, 978-283-1776, 7seaswhalewatch.com).

Captain Bill and Sons Whale Watch (24 Harbor Loop, 800-339-4253).

BEACHES

Good Harbor Beach (Thatcher Road/Route 127A). Good Harbor Beach is considered one of the most beautiful beaches in New England. Enjoy lots of good waves! Nonresidents need to make parking reservations online.

Wingaersheek Beach (232 Atlantic Street). The beach is good for sand-dollar hunting. Nonresidents need to make parking reservations online.

Cressy's Beach and **Half Moon Beach** (24 Hough Avenue). These beaches are located at Stage Fort Park. Nonresidents need to make parking reservations online.

Pavilion Beach (Stacy Boulevard). This beach is located along Stacy Boulevard on Western Avenue near the Fisherman's Memorial Statue. Enjoy sea-glass hunting!

Check out the official City of Gloucester website for additional beach and parking app information (gloucester-ma.gov/299/Beach-Information).

PARKS AND PLAYGROUNDS

Stage Fort Park (24 Hough Avenue). This beautiful park overlooks Gloucester's picturesque outer harbor. The park was named for the "stages" or wooden sheds and platforms which were used to dry cod; and the area was fortified as a "fort" for the first time in 1635. Stop by the excellent Visitor Center. Stage Fort Park has a very popular playground, two small beaches, a dog park, picnic tables, and two baseball fields. Look for the historic cannons, and visit the huge tablet rock which pays tribute to Gloucester as the first permanent settlement in the Massachusetts Bay Colony in 1623. Then look for the painting of a sea serpent on a rock on Cressy's Beach at the far end of the baseball field. Concerts are held at the Antonio Gentile Bandstand every Sunday night at 7 p.m. throughout the summer. Nonresidents need to make parking reservations online.

Benjamin Smith Playground (79 East Main Street). Located at Cripple Cove Landing, you will find swings, a jungle gym, benches, and a spectacular view of the harbor.

Gordon Thomas Playground (5 East Main Street).

Green Street Park (Doucette Playground; 10 Green Street).

Gemmellaro Ciaramitaro Playground (Fort Point; park at 110 Commercial Street).

Burnham Field Playground (9 Sargent Street).

LIGHTHOUSES

Annisquam Lighthouse (visible from Wingaersheek Beach). Annisquam Lighthouse, established in 1801, is one of the oldest lighthouses in America. It is famous for sightings of sea serpents and daring rescues along its rocky shores. This lighthouse is not open to the public but you can see it from Wingaersheek Beach.

Eastern Point Lighthouse (Eastern Point Road). This beautiful lighthouse, erected in 1832, is owned by the Coast Guard and is near the Massachusetts Audubon Eastern Point Wildlife Sanctuary. In front of the lighthouse is the Dog Bar breakwater made of huge granite blocks. You can walk out on the breakwater and look back to get a good view of the lighthouse. You can even do a little fishing or watch seashore birds, migrating birds, and butterflies. On a clear day, you can see the Boston skyline! Winslow Homer lived at this lighthouse and painted there in 1880. Parking is limited and free for Audubon members.

Ten Pound Island Lighthouse (Ten Pound Island). The historic lighthouse, located in Gloucester's Inner Harbor, opened in 1821. You can see it from Solomon Jacobs Park which is located at 8 Harbor Loop near the Coast Guard Station.

Read more about Ten Pound Island! While the name's origin isn't clear, it was most likely named for ten pens or "pounds" for sheep on the island. Another theory is that the Native American Indians were paid ten pounds for the island—about forty-eight dollars in American currency at the time. In the summer of 1880, Winslow Homer, one of the best-known painters of landscape and marine subjects, spent the summer at this lighthouse and produced over fifty paintings of Gloucester Harbor. In August 1817, Ten Pound Island became famous for many sightings of sea serpents. Amos Story, who later became the lighthouse keeper from 1833–1847, was one of the first citizens to report seeing the sea serpent in August 1817. He reported in a sworn statement, "It was between the hours of twelve and one o'clock when I first saw him and he continued in sight for about an hour and a half. I was setting on the shore and was about twenty rods [330 feet] from him when he was nearest to me. His head appeared shaped much like the head of a sea turtle and he carried his head from ten to twelve inches above the surface of the water. His head at that distance appeared larger than the head of any dog that I ever saw. From the back part of his head to the next part of him that was visible, I should judge to be three or four feet, he moved rapidly through the water, I should say a mile or two, at most, in three minutes. I saw no bunches on his back. On this day, I did not see more than ten or twelve feet of his body." Sea serpents continued to be seen in Gloucester Harbor until 1819.

WALKS AND HIKES

Stacy Boulevard (Western Ave). Enjoy a leisurely stroll along the ocean on Stacy Boulevard. This boulevard or esplanade was the vision of George Stacy who was a hotel man and the city's park commissioner in 1908. His dream of a walkway along the ocean became a reality in 1928. You will be amazed by the colorful flower gardens along the boulevard which were created, and are tended to, by the Generous Gardeners of Gloucester.

Be sure to visit the famous **Fisherman's Memorial Statue** and the **Fishermen's Wives Memorial**. See below for more details.

Walk down beyond the tennis courts and enjoy the **Elizabeth Gordon Smith Garden**.

See the lovely statue of **Triton**, created by Walker Hancock, an internationally known sculptor and long-time resident of Gloucester. Triton was the son of Poseidon, the Greek God of the Sea. It was believed that Triton could calm the seas by blowing his conch shell.

Stop at the **Blynman Bridge** and watch the boats try to maneuver their way through the canal which connects the Annisquam River to the harbor. It is not easy! The harbormaster commented on NBC TV, "This is a dangerous spot even for experienced boaters." On a busy summer day, the bridge will open over fifty to sixty times! The drawbridge is one of the busiest on the East Coast.

Read more about the Blynman Bridge! The "cut bridge" is named after the Reverend Richard Blynman, a minister and political leader. He supervised the digging of the first canal in 1643 which connected the Annisquam River and the Atlantic Ocean. Boats no longer had to make the dangerous trip around Cape Ann in the open ocean to get to Gloucester Harbor.

Harbor Walk (10 Rogers Street, gloucester.harborwalk.org). This is an award-winning, self-guided tour around Gloucester's harbor and downtown. It follows a series of forty-two granite posts. Each post tells a story of the site and shares a quote or photograph. Use your QRC code for videos. You will learn a lot of very interesting information. A map of the Harbor Walk is available online or at any one of the visitor centers.

Ravenswood Park (481 Western Avenue, thetrustees.org/place/ravenswood-park). There are ten miles of easy to moderate hiking trails in this park. Families especially enjoy the Ledge Hill Trail which is a two-mile loop. A map is available at the beginning of the trail or at the Visitor's Center at Stage Fort Park.

Dogtown Common (Dogtown Road, discovergloucester.com/directory/dogtown). Dogtown Common is a five-square-mile wooded area in Gloucester and Rockport. Take Dogtown Road off Cherry Street. The trails are not well marked so a map would be useful. During the Great Depression when so many people were out of work, Roger Babson, a Gloucester native, millionaire, and founder of Babson College, employed Finnish stone cutters to carve inspirational sayings on 24 large glacial-erratic boulders left by the receding ice in the Ice Age. You will see such sayings as: "Kindness," "Never Try, Never Win," "Save," "Get A Job," and "Loyalty."

MUSEUMS

Cape Ann Museum (27 Pleasant Street, 978-283-0455, capeannmuseum.org). This simply beautiful museum tells the story of Cape Ann. You can't miss the coiled sculpture of a sea serpent created by Chris Williams of Essex as you enter the museum; the sculpture commemorates the sea serpent seen swimming in Gloucester's inner harbor by hundreds of residents in August of 1817—pick up a "Cassie the Sea Serpent" brochure created especially for families. Families may also go on a fun scavenger hunt as they tour the Museum. Don't miss the impressive Fresnel lens and visit the fishing industry room to view an amazing film of fishing in the old days. On the first floor, you can view the cannonball which was fired by the British frigate *Falcon* off Norman's Woe during the War of 1812; it hit the steeple of the Universalist Church in Gloucester. The paintings in the Fitz Henry Lane room will give you an idea of what Gloucester Harbor looked like at the height of the fishing industry in the 1800s when there were up to four hundred beautiful schooners in Gloucester. Be sure to visit the gift shop before you leave!

Cape Ann Museum Green (13 Poplar Street, 978-283-0455, capeannmuseum.org/wec). In 2021, the Cape Ann Museum opened the Janet and William Ellery James Center at the Cape Ann Museum Green. Many different exhibitions are held there each year and you can visit three historical houses on the property.

Hammond Castle Museum (80 Hesperus Street, 978-283-2080, hammondcastle.org). Built between 1926 and 1929, the castle was the home and laboratory of extraordinary inventor John Hayes Hammond Jr. Nicknamed "The Father of Radio Control," Hammond was awarded more than 400 US patents. He was also awarded another 400 patents from other countries to make a total of 800 patents. This castle is made of granite cut from nearby quarries and has a drawbridge, interesting towers and turrets, and scary gargoyles. There is a huge pipe organ with 8,400 pipes inside. It is one of the largest pipe organs in the world. There are many fascinating 14th-, 15th-, and 16th-century artifacts from Hammond's collection for visitors to see. Pick up a scavenger-hunt sheet at the gift shop and look for things both inside the museum and outside in the beautiful gardens overlooking the ocean.

Beauport, the Sleeper-McCann House (75 Eastern Point Boulevard, 978-283-0800, historicnewengland.org/property/beauport-sleeper-mccann-house). This forty-room house was built by Henry David Sleeper in 1907. He was one of the first professional interior decorators in the United States. Henry used this house as a summer home to showcase his interior decorating ideas and to entertain his guests. Children can take a scavenger hunt in the house and around the beautiful gardens overlooking the ocean.

Sargent House Museum (49 Middle Street, 978-281-2432, sargenthouse.org). This beautiful Georgian style home was built in 1782 for Judith Sargent Murray (1751–1820) by her father, Winthrop Sargent, a successful Gloucester merchant. She lived here with her first husband John Stevens and then, after his death, with her second husband and the first minister of the Universalist Church in Gloucester, Reverend John Murray. This Universalist church was the first Universalist Church in the nation. In 1791, Judith wrote *On the Equality of the Sexes* which formed the first arguments for equal rights anywhere in the United States. She was also a poet, essayist, letter writer, and playwright. She believed women should have the right to be educated, have a marriage partnership, and paid work. See the tiny "writing closet" in the museum where Judith did her work. You can also see beautiful paintings by John Singer Sargent who was Judith Sargent's great-grand nephew. John Singer Sargent's sister Emily was also a painter; in 1998, 440 of her watercolor paintings were found in the attic of the Sargent family home in England—fifteen of the watercolor paintings were recently donated to the Sargent House Museum and will be on display in the near future. The Museum has a scavenger hunt that is sure to entertain children.

Maritime Gloucester (23 Harbor Loop, 978-281-0470, maritimegloucester.org). Families will enjoy the outdoor Sea-Pocket Aquarium touch tanks and the interactive exhibits inside. There is also a gift shop. You can walk out on the Harriet Webster Pier and watch the fishing boats coming in and out of the harbor; the schooners *Adventure* and *Ardelle* are berthed at this pier.

ART

Cape Ann Museum (27 Pleasant Street, 978-283-0455, capeannmuseum.org). Enjoy exquisite landscape and seascape paintings, Fitz Henry Lane's famous "painter of light" harbor paintings, beautiful family portraits, sculptures, the Folly Cove Designers block print art, furniture, decorative arts, fishing and marine art, and more! There is always a special art exhibition. Don't miss the sculpture garden in the courtyard and in the little park across the street. Check their website for ongoing family art programs. There are also many wonderful art exhibitions going on at Cape Ann Museum's new Janet and William Ellery James Center at 13 Poplar Street.

City Hall (9 Dale Avenue, 978-281-9700, gloucester-ma.gov. Gloucester's magnificent City Hall was built in 1870. It is one of the oldest working city halls in Massachusetts. Take the stairs to the second landing and you will see the Fishermen's Memorial Wall which lists the names of the fishermen lost at sea from 1894–1978. According to the Massachusetts Cultural Council, the Gloucester City Hall has the best Works Progress Administration murals in Massachusetts. In 1935, when so many people were out of work because of the Great Depression, the FAP, or the Federal Arts Project (a branch of the Works Progress Administration), hired artists who came to City Hall to paint ten colorful murals. You can see the murals on the walls of the first and second floors in City Hall. The artists were Frederick Mulhaupt, Oscar Anderson, Charles Allen Winter, and Charles Stoddard. And don't miss the portrait of Howard Blackburn!

Read more about Howard Blackburn! *In 1883, Howard Blackburn and his dory mate were fishing off the fishing vessel* Grace L. Fears *when a storm came up. They lost sight of their mother ship and were lost at sea. Howard's dory mate died but Howard decided to row to the nearest shore which was Newfoundland. He lost his mittens and realized he would need to curve his hands around the oars and let them freeze in place if he was going to make it to shore. He made it to shore after five days without sleep, food, or water. He was well cared for by the people of Newfoundland but did lose all his fingers and some toes. In the spring of 1884, he returned to Gloucester a hero and opened the Blackburn Tavern. The original building is at 289 Main Street and is now a restaurant. Howard went on to make two solo Atlantic Crossings! He sailed from Gloucester in 1899 on a 30-foot sloop called the* Great Western *and reached Gloucester, England, in 62 days. In 1903 he sailed to Portugal on the 25-foot sloop* Great Republic *and reached Portugal in 39 days. You can see the* Great Republic *at Cape Ann Museum.*

North Shore Art Association (11 Pirates Lane, 978-283-1857, nsarts.org). Enjoy the outstanding art exhibitions while overlooking Gloucester's inner harbor and Rocky Neck Art Colony!

Rocky Neck Art Colony (Rocky Neck Avenue, 978-515-7004, rockyneckartcolony.org). Part of Gloucester's Rocky Neck Cultural District, Rocky Neck Art Colony is the oldest continuously operating art colony in America. Stroll along Rocky Neck Avenue and enjoy galleries filled with paintings, jewelry, and pottery. Nearby, you will find good restaurants and ice cream. You can ride the *Gloucester Harbor Water Shuttle & Tour* from downtown Gloucester to Rocky Neck and back, or drive and park on Rocky Neck Avenue. At the end of Rocky Neck Avenue is the Gloucester Marine Railways which was established in 1859 and is one of the oldest continuously operating shipyards in the United States. It is here where fishing boats, commercial boats, and pleasure boats are maintained and repaired.

Rocky Neck Cultural Center (6 Wonson Street, 978-515-7004, rockyneckartcolony.org). Open year round, this unique and historic Carpenter Gothic building is the "home base" for the Rocky Neck Art Colony. Built in 1877, it was used as a neighborhood meeting house and a church. At the turn of the century, famous artists like Winslow Homer, Edward Hopper, and Childe Hassam painted here. In 2014, the building became the home of many fine art exhibitions, lectures, and workshops.

Rocky Neck Historic Art Trail (Rocky Neck Avenue, 978-515-7004, trail. rockyneckartcolony.org). There are fifteen sites historically significant to art in and around Rocky Neck Avenue that are associated with artists featured in a book by Judith Curtis called *Rocky Neck Art Colony 1850–1950*. Start at the public parking lot on Rocky Neck Avenue. Download a map available online before you go!

Cape Pond Ice Co (104 Commercial Street, 978-283-0174, capepondice.com). Cape Pond Ice first began supplying ice to Gloucester's fishing boats in 1848. Originally, ice was cut from local ponds using huge ice saws. Before that, fish were preserved in salt or brine. With the advent of refrigeration, ice was manufactured inside plants like Cape Pond Ice. As Sebastian Junger writes in his book *The Perfect Storm*, "Commercial fishing wouldn't be possible without ice, there is simply no other way to get fish to market." Fishing vessels used to pull up to the wharf at Cape Pond Ice and load 300 pounds to 30 tons of ice per fishing trip. These days Cape Pond Ice is a smaller ice production facility and only sells bagged ice. They are no longer offering tours, but it is worth stopping by to see a short movie about the history of ice making and to visit the gift shop. You can buy a "Coolest Guys Around" T-shirt made famous by the character Bugsy in *The Perfect Storm*.

MEMORIAL STATUES

Joan of Arc Statue (10 Washington Street). This magnificent bronze statue of Joan of Arc on horseback was created by Anna Hyatt Huntington (1876–1973). Anna was a summer resident of the Gloucester village of Annisquam where she had a studio. The statue was commissioned by the French Government and presented to the City of Gloucester with gratitude for the soldiers who gave their lives in World War I fighting along with the French. Dedicated in 1921, the statue is located at the traffic circle at the corner of Washington and Middle Streets and faces the American Legion Hall. The model for the horse was Frank, a Perchero, or draft horse, that was part of the East Gloucester Fire Station horse team. Anna's niece posed as Joan. Anna went on to become very famous for her animal sculptures which can be seen in many museums in this country and in Europe.

Fitz Henry Lane Sculpture (8 Harbor Loop). The statue of the famous luminist painter or painter of light, Fitz Henry Lane (1804–1865), is located on a hill along with Lane's granite home in Captain Solomon Jacobs Park, overlooking the harbor and Maritime Gloucester Museum. Notice the crutches on the ground; it is believed that Fitz Henry Lane may have had polio. Alfred Duca, a nationally known artist and sculptor who lived in Annisquam, created this statue and gave it to the City of Gloucester. He wanted to honor Fitz Henry Lane and all the artists who came to Gloucester over the years to paint.

Fisherman's Memorial Statue (Stacy Boulevard). This famous statue pays tribute to the fishermen of Gloucester. Leonard F. Craske was the sculptor and won the competition to design a memorial for Gloucester's 300th Anniversary in 1923. The model for the statue was a local fisherman.

Fishermen's Wives Memorial (Stacy Boulevard). Morgan Faulds Pike was the sculptor of this beautiful bronze statue, and Ann Gilardi Johnson designed the site with the meditative benches and four entries reflecting the points on a compass. The statue was dedicated on August 5, 2001 by the Fishermen's Wives Association. The paving stones around the statue read, "The Wives, Mothers, Daughters and Sisters of Gloucester Fishermen and Mariners Everywhere for Their Faith, Diligence and Fortitude." The Fishermen's Wives Association was the leader in envisioning the statue. The project was funded with many small donations.

FESTIVALS

Saint Peter's Fiesta (2 Commercial Street, stpetersfiesta.org). For 96 years, the festival has been held in late June commemorating Saint Peter. Read all about the Fiesta in Alice Gardner's first book *Saint Peter's Fiesta*, available on Amazon and at The Bookstore of Gloucester at 61 Main Street.

Gloucester Schooner Festival (maritimegloucester.org/schooner-festival). Hosted by Maritime Gloucester, more than 25 elegant schooners come to Gloucester Harbor to honor the major role schooners played in the fishing industry of Gloucester. The event is held Labor Day weekend. The Parade of Sail is on Sunday morning. Gloucester is represented by the *Adventure*, the *Ardelle*, the *Thomas E. Lannon*, the *Bald Eagle*, the *Green Dragon*, and the *Strombus*.

Ongoing Events (goodmorninggloucester.com/cape-ann-arts-calendar). Take a look at Joey Ciaramitaro's famous award-winning blog *Good Morning Gloucester: My View of Life on the Dock* for the latest Gloucester news and happenings.

ABOUT THE AUTHOR AND ILLUSTRATOR

Alice has had an art studio in Gloucester for many years. During this time, she has gotten to know and love Gloucester and its people. She is constantly amazed at all the unique things to see and do in the small, seaside city. She decided to publish an alphabet book of paintings for all ages, highlighting the beauty of Gloucester and all it has to offer.

"Let's Explore Gloucester!" in the back of the book is designed to help young families discover activities in Gloucester.

Alice is also the author and illustrator of *Saint Peter's Fiesta, Gloucester, Massachusetts* and *Fourth of July, Manchester-By-The Sea.*

ACKNOWLEDGEMENTS

Thank you to the late Mary Sue Wonson, my writing buddy of over forty years; before her death in February 2022, she helped me persevere with this book and offered much encouragement. Thanks to her husband, Roger Wonson, who offered many helpful suggestions.

Thank you to the staff at Cape Ann Museum whose interest in and enthusiasm for the book helped me bring it over the finish line.

Thank you to my granddaughter Anna Gardner. During the first year of the pandemic in 2020, we met at four o'clock every day over Zoom to paint together and encourage each other. It was during that year that I began and completed the forty-six paintings for this book.

Thank you to my friend Annamarie Lavieri who gave me the idea for the letter Z—Zuppa which is Italian for soup. She also helped review the manuscript and offered much interest in the book.

Thank you to the staff at Hammond Castle; Beauport, the Sleeper-McCann House; the Sargent House Museum; and Cape Pond Ice Co. for being so generous with their time as I searched for ways to interest children in these special places.

Thanks to my friends Carol McKenna, Barbara Amero, Gail Pease, and Lorraine Cooper for their wonderful support.

Thanks to my husband David who always believed in me.

This book would not be possible without the unwavering positive energy and great work of my editor, Damaris Curran Herlihy with Curran Press, and Cathy Kelley, my very innovative and creative designer. Thank you!

REFERENCES

Beauport, the Sleeper-McCann House

"Beauport, the Sleeper-McCann House." New England Museum Association. nemanet.org/museums/beauport-sleeper-mccann-house.

Blynman Bridge

"Blynman Bridge." The Historical Marker Database. hmdb.org/m.asp?m=36363.

Cape Pond Ice

"Cape Pond Ice History & Photos." Cape Pond Ice. capepondice.com/cape-pond-ice-history.

"Cape Pond Ice, Gloucester, Since 1848" [Brochure].

City Hall

"Gloucester City Hall: Winter Murals—Gloucester MA." The Living New Deal. livingnewdeal.org/projects/gloucester-city-hall-civic-virtues-mural-gloucester-ma.

"City Hall." Gloucester Harbor Walk. gloucester.harborwalk.org/story-posts/sp-11.

Eastern Point Lighthouse

"Eastern Point Lighthouse." Lighthousefriends.com. lighthousefriends.com/light.asp?ID=476.

"Eastern Point Lighthouse." New England Lighthouses: A Virtual Guide. newenglandlighthouses.net/eastern-point-lighthouse.

Fishermen's Wives Memorial

"Fisherman's Wives Memorial, Gloucester, MA." Flickr. flickr.com/photos/bootbearwdc/2660885263.

"Gloucester Fishermen's Wives Memorial Celebrates 20th Anniversary." Northshore Magazine. nshoremag.com/arts-culture/gloucester-fishermens-wives-memorial-celebrates-20th-anniversary.

"The Fishermen's Memorial and Fishermen's Wives Memorial (Gloucester Harbor): Location, History, and Legends." North Shore Community College. https://appsprod.northshore.edu/poetry/gloucester/memorialshistory.htm.

Fitz Henry Lane

"Fitz Henry Lane." Wikipedia. en.wikipedia.org/wiki/Fitz_Henry_Lane.

"Fitz Henry Lane." Gloucester Harbor Walk. gloucester.harborwalk.org/story-posts/sp-18.

Hammond Castle

"John Hays Hammond, Jr.—Father of Radio Control." EE Times. eetimes.com/john-hays-hammond-jr-father-of-radio-control.

"Hammond Castle." Wikipedia. en.wikipedia.org/wiki/Hammond_Castle.

"History of Hammond Castle." History of Massachusetts Blog. historyofmassachusetts.org/the-history-of-hammond-castle.

Howard Blackburn

"Captain Howard Blackburn, the Lone Voyager." Cape Ann Museum. capeannmuseum.org/howard-blackburn.

"The Terrible Odyssey Of Howard Blackburn," American Heritage. americanheritage.com/terrible-odyssey-howard-blackburn.

Joan of Arc

"Anna Hyatt Huntington: World War I Memorial to the Sons of Gloucester." Isabella Stewart Gardner Museum. gardnermuseum.org/blog/anna-hyatt-huntington-world-war-i-memorial-sons-gloucester.

"Joan of Arc." Gloucester Harbor Walk. gloucester.harborwalk.org/story-posts/sp-37.

Jodrey State Fish Pier

"Jodrey State Fish Pier (Gloucester Harbor): Location, History, and Legends." North Shore Community College. appsprod.northshore.edu/poetry/gloucester/fishpierhistory.htm.

Sargent House

"About Us." The Sargent House Museum. sargenthouse.org/about.

"Sargent House Museum." The History List. thehistorylist.com/venues/sargent-house-museum-gloucester-massachusetts.

Schooner Adventure

Schooner Adventure at Maritime Gloucester. schooner-adventure.org.

Schooner Ardelle

"The Ardelle's debut." Gloucester Daily Times. gloucestertimes.com/news/local_news/the-ardelles-debut/article_d65f726d-3e6f-566d-8b8e-52760ea61d7a.html.

"Essex shipwright, schooner showcased." The Salem News. salemnews.com/news/essex-shipwright-schooner-showcased/article_c7c5b6e8-893f-5d5a-a36f-beedfaeaa0af.html.

Schooner Thomas E. Lannon

"About the Boat." Schooner Sails. schooner.org/about-the-boat.

Stacy Boulevard

"Stacy Esplanade." The Historical Marker Database. hmdb.org/m.asp?m=36360.

"Stacy Boulevard History Lives On." Good Morning Gloucester. goodmorninggloucester.com/2021/08/20/stacy-boulevard-history-lives-on.

Stage Fort Park

"Stage Fort Park—Gloucester Visitor Center." Essex Coastal Scenic Byway. coastalbyway.org/communities/gloucester/stage-fort-park-gloucester-visitor-center.

"Parks and Recreational Facilities: Stage Fort Park." City of Gloucester. gloucester-ma.gov/450/Parks-and-Recreational-Facilities.

Ten Pound Island

"Ten Pound Island Lighthouse." Lighthousefriends.com. lighthousefriends.com/light.asp?ID=478.

"Ten Pound Island Light." National Park Service. nps.gov/nr/travel/maritime/ten.htm.

Triton Statue

"Triton Sculpture—Gloucester, MA." Waymarking. waymarking.com/waymarks/wm80D5_Triton_Sculpture_Gloucester_MA.